Stephen Stands Strong

The Story of Stephen, the First Christian Martyr
Acts 6:5–7:60 for children

Written by Julie Stiegemeyer
Illustrated by Glenn Myers

Arch® Books
Copyright © 2001 Concordia Publishing House
3558 S. Jefferson Avenue, St. Louis, MO 63118-3968
Manufactured in the United States of America

Jesus died to forgive our sin,
Then rose on Easter morn.
His friends believed, the message spread,
And the Christian church was born.

Jesus sent out the apostles,
Sharing His Word far and near.
They preached the message of God's love
For all the people to hear.

Stephen trusted in God's strong love.
He also wanted to tell
About the work of Jesus Christ
And His love with man to dwell.

Stephen watched the apostles work;
So many needed care.
Who could assist them in their task—
God's saving Word to share?

They wanted to find some helpers
To serve the needy and poor.
So seven deacons were chosen
To spread God's Word some more.

Stephen was one of the seven;
His work began right away.
He showed the people God's power
And taught God's gracious ways.

Some men disagreed with Stephen
And said his teaching was wrong.
Jesus was not God's Son, they said,
And they argued all day long.

So Stephen explained with wisdom
How God had worked of old
To show how He loved His people
Through prophets brave and bold.

Stephen described how Abraham
Trusted God's wonderful plan.
He became father to Isaac
As he lived in the Promised Land.

He also talked about Joseph
And troubles that made him sad.
But Joseph believed and trusted
That God could bring good from bad.

God called Moses to lead the way
So Israel could be freed.
As he walked through the dry Red Sea,
God was all that he would need.

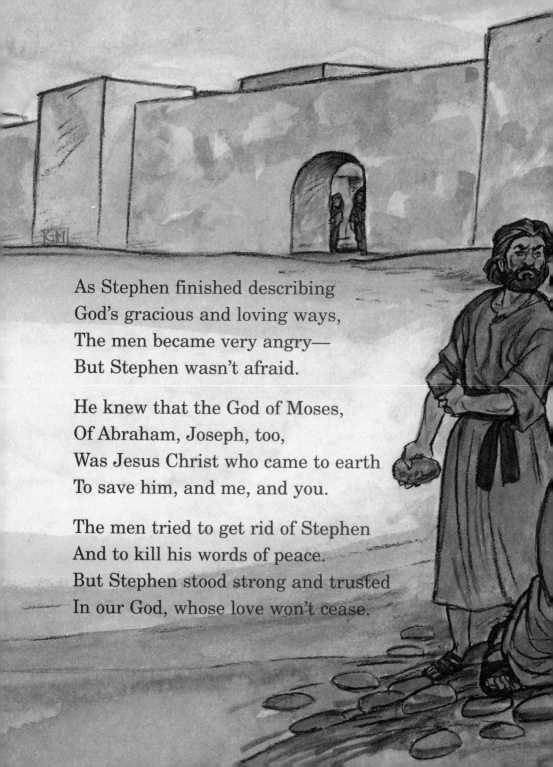

As Stephen finished describing
God's gracious and loving ways,
The men became very angry—
But Stephen wasn't afraid.

He knew that the God of Moses,
Of Abraham, Joseph, too,
Was Jesus Christ who came to earth
To save him, and me, and you.

The men tried to get rid of Stephen
And to kill his words of peace.
But Stephen stood strong and trusted
In our God, whose love won't cease.

So also will God embrace you.
He will shield you with His love.
Even when your life is over,
You'll go to heaven above.

Let what you say about Jesus
Be as wise and brave and bold
As Stephen's defense of Jesus
And God's mercy from of old.

Dear Parents,

Stephen stood strong in his faith. Amid accusations and danger, his faith in Jesus did not waver. The biblical account reports that the angry crowd mobbed, then stoned Stephen. He was faithful unto death—an example for us all. What would you and I do if we faced similar circumstances?

While we might not face stoning in our lifetime, there are Christians around the world who face persecution because they stand strong and do not hide their faith. Why? Because they live forgiven and strengthened through the blood of Christ on the cross.

Stephen found the Good News of God's love through Jesus too important to remain silent. Do you and your child know someone who needs to hear this good news? Is there a way for you to witness your faith to family members and friends? Invite them to attend church and Sunday school with you. Let them know you are praying for them in their time of need. Give a Bible as a gift, and mark your favorite passages. Like Stephen, we too can stand strong in our faith—guided and strengthened through Christ.

The Editor